D0001924

Conquering the
Fatigue, Depression,
&Weight Gain
Caused by
Low Thyroid

VALERIE
SAXION

Strength
& Honor

BRONZE BOW PUBLISHING
www.bronzebowpublishing.com

BOOKS BY VALERIE SAXION

The Easy Way to Regain and Maintain Your Perfect Weight
Every Body Has Parasites
How to Detoxify and Renew Your Body From Within
How to Feel Great All the Time
How to Stop Candida and Other Yeast Conditions
    in Their Tracks

The information in this book is for educational purposes only and is not recommended as a means of diagnosing or treating an illness. Neither the publisher nor author is engaged in rendering professional advice or services to the individual reader. All matters regarding physical and mental health should be supervised by a health practitioner knowledgeable in treating that particular condition. Neither the author nor the publisher shall be liable or responsible for any loss, injury, or damage allegedly arising from any information or suggestion in this book.

Conquering the Fatigue, Depression, and Weight Gain
Caused by Low Thyroid
Copyright © 2003 Valerie Saxion

All Scripture quotations, unless otherwise indicated, are taken from the *Holy Bible, New International Version®*. NIV®. Copyright © 1973, 1978, 1984 by International Bible Society. Used by permission of Zondervan Publishing House. All rights reserved.

ISBN 0-9724563-9-2

Published by Bronze Bow Publishing, Inc., 2600 East 26th Street, Minneapolis, MN 55406.

You can reach us on the Internet
at www.bronzebowpublishing.com.

Literary development and cover/interior design by Koechel Peterson & Associates, Inc., Minneapolis, Minnesota.

Manufactured in the United States of America

CONTENTS

ABOUT THE AUTHOR

DR. VALERIE SAXION IS ONE OF America's most articulate champions of nutrition and spiritual healing. A twenty-year veteran of health science with a primary focus in Naturopathy, Valerie has a delightful communication style and charming demeanor that will open your heart, clear your mind, and uplift you to discover abundant natural health God's way.

As the co-founder of Valerie Saxion's Silver Creek Labs, a manufacturer and distributor of nutritional supplements and health products, Dr. Saxion has seen firsthand the power of God's remedies as the sick are healed and the lame walk.

Valerie is seen regularly on the weekly Trinity Broadcasting Network program *On Call* that airs worldwide on TBN, Sky Angel, Daystar, and the Health & Healing television networks. She has been interviewed on numerous radio talk shows as well as television appearances.

Hosts love to open the line for callers to phone in their health concerns while Dr. Saxion gives on-the-air advice and instruction.

Dr. Saxion has also lectured at scores of health events nationwide and in Canada. After attending one of her lectures, you will leave empowered with the tools to live and love in a healthy body!

To schedule Dr. Saxion for a lecture or interview, please contact Joy at 1-800-493-1146, or fax 817-236-5411, or email at: valeriesaxon@cs.com.

Married to Jim Saxion for twenty-plus years, they are the parents of eight healthy children, ages 1 to 21.

WHAT IS HYPOTHYROIDISM?

MANY YEARS AGO A MAN WALKED into my health food store and went to the shelf that displayed our weight-loss products. I watched as he searched over our variety of brands, and soon it was obvious from the frustrated look on his face that he was not finding what he was looking for.

"How may I help you?" I asked, walking down the aisle to give him some assistance.

"Well, I can't find this brand," he replied, showing me a bottle of a diet product that I wasn't familiar with, "so I'm afraid I'm out of luck. I used this a few years back, and it really helped me take off the weight. I've tried and tried to find something similar, but . . . nothing else has ever worked the same—not even close. I've tried these other brands, believe me."

"That's odd," I said as I took the bottle from his hand. "There must a reason why this worked for you. Give me a minute to check it out."

I then began comparing every ingredient in the old bottle with the other weight-loss products on the shelf. All the ingredients were basically the same except for one notable difference. The old diet product contained an herbal remedy called bladder wrack that was lacking in any of the new products.

"Okay, I think I might be able to help you," I said, handing him back his bottle. "If you combine one of these diet products with a liquid bladder wrack, which was in the original product that worked for you, that should do it."

"Bladder wrack. What's that?" he asked, looking a bit skeptical.

"It's an herb made from a brown seaweed," I answered. "It's all natural to the body, and it's excellent for speeding up the metabolism. No bad side effects. Give it a try."

He did so and within two weeks he was losing weight again, plus he said he was starting to feel good and was mentally excited.

This man's weight problem and general malaise was due to a low thyroid condition that he was totally unaware of! Once the bladder wrack had sped up his metabolism, his body was able to burn the calories that were giving him a problem.

AVERAGE DOES NOT MEAN HEALTHY

It happens in doctors' offices untold times every day of the week. A woman comes in for a consultation, saying she's finally had it with her weight problem and fatigue. No matter what new diet she tries, nothing works. Even her "fat clothes" no longer fit. She's desperate to fix it, but what can be done?

An observant doctor should immediately notice that the woman's skin is dry and flaky, and her hair is coarse and thin. If he shakes her hand, he should note that it feels icy cold. All of which, along with the weight-loss problem and nagging fatigue, are symptoms of a low thyroid condition. Unfortunately, often these signals are overlooked.

"Tell me more about what you're feeling," she is asked.

"Oh, I don't know, but there's got to be something radically wrong with me," she says with a deep sigh. "No matter what I try, I keep putting on the weight. And every time I try to diet and exercise, I fall apart. I get so bone-tired

I can hardly move, even when I've had a good night's rest. And I'm grouchy all the time— everything seems to bother me. It didn't used to be like this. I'm so beat out I don't even care anymore."

After more discussion she is run through the standard lab tests, which eventually come back and suggest that everything looks pretty much normal. All too often she is then told that what she is experiencing is a common complaint from scores of patients, and she is in fact perfectly normal. While the words are not spoken, she walks away with the impression that it must be in her head.

She is in fact, fairly *average*. Millions of men and women, but especially women, suffer with underactive thyroid glands that suppress their metabolism. But *average* does not mean healthy, and it's certainly not *normal*. The fact that a person has no energy and can't keep the weight off are clear symptoms of someone who has a health problem.

HYPOTHYROIDISM

Although it weighs only a mere two-thirds of an ounce, the thyroid gland is the largest gland in the neck and is phenomenally important to your overall health. Located in the front of your neck below the skin and muscle layers, this gland has the shape of a butterfly with wings, which represent the left and right thyroid lobes that wrap around the trachea. Every hour of every day approximately five quarts of blood circulate through your thyroid gland, delivering iodide (a compound of iodine) to the gland as well as hormones from the pituitary gland that stimulate the thyroid into production. Iodide is the material your thyroid gland uses to make its hormone.

Your thyroid gland makes, stores, and releases the thyroid hormone directly into your bloodstream for delivery to your cells wherever and whenever it is needed. The thyroid hormone has a vital effect on nearly all the tissues of your body by increasing cellular activity. This function regulates your body's metabolism (the rate your body utilizes oxygen) and is, therefore, responsible for keeping every cell and tissue in the body healthy. The thyroid controls the rate at which your various organs function and the speed at which your body burns the nutrients you supply it.

Basically, it controls your immune system, which represents the body's ability to resist disease. Can you imagine such a tiny gland having such an awesome function!

When your body lacks sufficient thyroid hormone, the condition is called hypothyroidism. Since the main purpose of the thyroid hormone is to drive the body's metabolism, it makes sense that people with this condition will experience symptoms associated with a slow metabolism. A body with insufficient thyroid hormone behaves much like a clock that no one winds up. It becomes tired and rundown. You can almost feel the organs slowing down. As your metabolism slows and burns fewer and fewer calories, it's no surprise if you experience a corresponding gain in weight. Difficulty with mental concentration intensifies as the brain slows down its functions. And constipation becomes a problem as the gut becomes sluggish. Your body was not meant to operate at such a slow metabolism. But don't be fooled by the fact that many potential symptoms can pop up. They can still be linked to the one source—low thyroid.

I hope you understand that hypothyroidism will often mask its symptoms effectively beneath other ailments; therefore, it often goes undiagnosed. Many of the symptoms of low thyroid are subtle because they are experienced commonly by people without thyroid deficiencies. Thus, many doctors may correctly and consistently note their patients' fatigue, weight gain, and/or depression, but incorrectly attribute those symptoms automatically to other causes. Physicians should always check to see if thyroid disease is the cause of these everyday symptoms.

Today, hypothyroidism is far more common than most people realize . . . and millions of people are currently hypothyroid and don't even know it! It is a condition that can occur in both males and females at any age, although middle-aged women are by far the highest percentage of those who are afflicted by the condition.

Left untreated, hypothyroidism can lead to a condition as seemingly benign as low body temperature and as complex and dangerous as heart failure, and, ultimately, to a condition known as myxedema coma, which is potentially fatal. But patients who are diagnosed and treated for an underactive thyroid can easily regain full control of their lives and eliminate these symptoms entirely. That is very good news!

SYMPTOMS AND CAUSES OF HYPOTHYROIDISM

THE SYMPTOMS OF LOW THYROID are mainly dependent on the amount of decrease in the thyroid hormone and how long the shortage has existed. For most patients, the symptoms are mild and may include the following:

- Significant fatigue and weakness
- Muscle swelling or cramps (mainly in the arms and legs)
- Intolerance to cold
- Frequent bouts of cold and influenza
- Weight gain or increased difficulty losing weight
- Dry, rough pale skin
- Coarse hair and hair loss, including eyebrows
- Chronic recurrent infection(s)
- Loss of appetite
- Constipation despite adequate dietary fiber
- Slowed pulse, delivering less blood to the tissues

- Low blood pressure
- Brittle nails that crack and peel easily
- Anemia, especially the B12 deficiency type
- Depression, irritability, and mood swings
- Problems with memory, focus, or concentration
- Hoarseness for no particular reason
- Abnormal menstrual cycles and severe PMS
- Loss of equilibrium
- Enlarged thyroid causing a lump in the neck
- Wounds that heal slowly
- Infertility or miscarriages
- Asthma and allergies
- Yellow-orange coloration in the skin, particularly in the palms of the hands
- Yellow bumps on the eyelids
- Slow speech
- Decreased libido
- Frequent headaches and migraines
- Burning or tingling in the fingers
- Arthritis
- Milky discharge from the breasts
- Fluid infiltration of the tissues causing puffiness (mainly in the face)

Any of these symptoms may represent a low thyroid condition. People vary in just what functions are diminished most when their thyroid hormone is low, and the number of these symptoms can vary with the severity of the deficiency. You may have only one symptom as your main complaint, while other people experience a combination of symptoms. There is no "one size fits all" regarding the symptoms, which can range from annoying to disabling. Occasionally, some patients with hypothyroidism have no symptoms at all, or they are so subtle they go unnoticed.

CAUSES OF HYPOTHYROIDISM

Low thyroid symptoms occur when your body tissues do not get enough of the thyroid hormone, apparently because of disrupted assembly within the thyroid gland. Therefore, understanding how your thyroid gland works and *why* your body's most important endocrine gland slows its production at the very moment when its full operation is required is important.

Think of your thyroid gland as the energy switch for your entire body. The hormone it secretes goes directly into your bloodstream and enters every cell. Because of the presence of that hormone in your cell, a complex protein molecule binds to DNA in a different manner than it would if that thyroid hormone were not there. This entire implementation functions like a switch to turn your cellular machinery on or off. In doing this, it regulates your cell temperature, function, and growth. When your thyroid gland malfunctions and reduces the amount of hormone it is releasing, your cellular machinery will correspondingly slow down. It slows down, symptoms begin to surface, often starting with a general fatigue that just doesn't go away even when you're well rested.

I hope you can picture that in your mind, because it will help motivate you to take action to remedy the problem. There's a cause or causes for this happening, which need to be resolved.

Dietary

Worldwide, the cause of most low thyroid function occurs when a person is not consuming enough iodine to make sufficient quantities of thyroid hormones to fuel the body cells. In the United States, however, extra iodine is put into various food items, including table salt and bread dough, nearly eliminating it as a cause for low thyroid function.

HASHIMOTO'S THYROIDITIS

The most common cause of hypothyroidism in the United States is *chronic autoimmune* thyroiditis (or *Hashimoto's thyroiditis*), a condition characterized by inflammation and damage to the thyroid tissue. Immune cells that routinely fight off infection and colds attack the body's own thyroid tissue instead, leaving a large percentage of the cells of the thyroid damaged or dead and incapable of producing sufficient hormone. As strange as it may seem, common low thyroid is a mild immune system illness.

OTHER AUTOIMMUNE DISEASES

If you have other autoimmune diseases, you may also be at risk for Hashimoto's thyroiditis. Rheumatoid arthritis (where immune cells attack the joints) and diabetes (where immune cells attack the pancreas, which produces insulin) are two such autoimmune diseases to watch. In fact, about 10 percent of patients with Type I or juvenile diabetes mellitus develop chronic thyroiditis sometime during their life. It is therefore important for diabetics to be checked regularly for thyroid disease. Other examples of autoimmune diseases include vitiligo (a skin disorder where patches of skin become white), Addison's disease (a disorder of the adrenal glands), and pernicious anemia (a particular form of low blood count).

TOXINS TO THE LIVER

The chemicals that make up the thyroid hormones are made in the liver. It makes sense that whatever inhibits the function of the liver will effect the production of the thyroid. According to *Mosby's Diagnostic and Laboratory Test Reference,* products such as aspirin, acetomenaphin, and over-the-counter pain medications lead to a sluggish thyroid function. Hormones, such as birth control, hormone replacement, etc., and steroids inhibit the production of the thyroid hormone as relates to the liver. If you have a problem with constipation, the liver is forced to work twice as hard and will slow the thyroid hormone production. These cause the thyroid to become sluggish, not necessarily diseased.

SURGERY

Whenever the thyroid gland is removed completely by surgery for whatever reason, hypothyroidism naturally results. Your doctor will prescribe medication to replace the hormone your body can no longer produce. If only half of your thyroid is removed and the remaining half is normal, you can still produce enough thyroid hormone in order to function normally. In this case, you need to have regular blood tests in order to make certain the remaining portion of the thyroid is functioning well. If it is not, you will need to start thyroid hormone medication.

AGING

Unfortunately, as we age, hypothyroidism becomes increasingly common, particularly in women. It is my personal opinion that aging is not the problem, but that many people experience a buildup of toxins that causes the liver to be sluggish and diminishes the production of the thyroid hormone. Therefore, if you are older, you should especially consider the "Liver Cleanse" that is described in the "Treatment of Hypothyroidism" chapter that follows.

PREGNANCY

Low thyroid is especially common in the postpartum period and easily confused with postpartum depression. You may require thyroid hormone adjustments. It is also important to note that both hypothyroidism and hyperthyroidism can sometimes cause unexplained infertility or miscarriages. Therefore, thyroid tests are often a routine part of evaluating a patient who has problems with pregnancy. In addition, the requirements for thyroid hormone may increase during pregnancy and should be monitored closely in the first and second trimester.

LITHIUM MEDICATION

If you are taking a prescription medication that has been shown to cause thyroid disease, you may be at risk for an underactive thyroid. Lithium, for instance, can cause thyroid enlargement and an underproduction of thyroid hormone.

Radioactive Iodine

Another cause of hypothyroidism is the use of radioactive iodine. Some thyroid diseases such as Graves' disease (a form of hyperthyroidism) are treated with radioactive iodine. The radioactive iodine destroys the overactive thyroid cells, thus eliminating the cause of hyperthyroidism. But the destruction of these cells sometimes goes too far and results in hypothyroidism. If you have been treated with therapeutic doses of radioactive iodine, you should visit your doctor regularly and have routine blood tests. In some cases, a small amount of thyroid tissue is not destroyed and produces enough thyroid hormone for the body for a little while. However, if this piece of thyroid burns out or gives up, hypothyroidism will result.

Secondary Hypothyroidism

Finally, there are some rare causes of hypothyroidism related to brain diseases, also called secondary hypothyroidism. Disorders of the pituitary gland or hypothalamus portions of the brain may cause thyroid hormone deficiency in addition to other hormonal imbalances. This type of rare hypothyroidism can also be treated with thyroid hormone medication.

DIAGNOSIS OF HYPOTHYROIDISM

SINCE HYPOTHYROIDISM IS CAUSED BY insufficient thyroid hormone being secreted into the bloodstream, its diagnosis is often based exclusively upon the measurement of the amount of thyroid hormone present in the blood. Years of testing have established normal ranges for the general population. If your hormone levels drop below the normal range, it's a good indication that you may be suffering from hypothyroidism. These tests are routinely available to anyone.

However, it's not always as simple as a test score. While some people may be diagnosed with these simple blood tests, most are not. Because the vast majority of low thyroid cases are caused by the autoimmune response involving an attack on your thyroid gland, the gland itself and blood tests may not show any abnormalities.

My husband, Jim, went for five years with

several symptoms of hypothyroidism, but his blood work said his levels were fine. Finally, after five years a doctor said to him, "Well, you have all the symptoms, so let's try the medication." Within days, Jim was like a new man.

The fact is that standard lab tests are unable to identify millions of borderline low thyroid sufferers. H. Jack Baskin, M.D., vice-president of the American Association of Clinical Endocrinologists, says, "While extreme hypothyroidism is rare and is easily identified, mild cases are often not detected in routine blood tests, so subclinical hypothyroidism mostly falls through the cracks. Your doctor might try to convince you that your symptoms are 'a normal part of aging' or 'nothing to worry about.' Don't buy it. It's your quality of life that is being severely compromised, and it is your right to get to the bottom of these 'minor' ailments."

Some doctors say that the blood work for the thyroid is only 20 percent effective. But some doctors only go by the blood results. Others only go by the symptoms. My recommendation is that if you have the symptoms, you find a doctor who will listen. The goal is not necessarily to improve the lab scores, but to make you feel better!

THE BARNES BASAL TEMPERATURE TEST

Since the thyroid gland controls your metabolism, one simple measure of your metabolic rate is your body temperature, which can be observed by both you and your physician. Over fifty years ago, Dr. Broda Barnes, a famous thyroid doctor with nearly fifty years of clinical practice, said, "More information can be brought to the physician with only the aid of an ordinary thermometer than can be attained with all other thyroid function tests combined." Fifty years have not changed the validity of his statement. He studied 1,569 patients over a period of twenty years to determine the role of thyroid deficiency in heart disease, and his discoveries led him to write a book called *Hypothyroidism: The Unsuspected Illness.*

In his book, Dr. Barnes states that 40 percent of Americans suffer from an inadequate supply of thyroid hormone. He noted that hypothyroidism often goes undiagnosed because blood thyroid values are usually inaccurate. He recommended a simple test, called the Barnes Basal Temperature Test, which you can easily perform at home.

Dr. Barnes found the basal temperature to be one of the most valid tests to evaluate thyroid function. The temperature test should be done immediately upon awakening in the morning and before you get out of bed. Here are the specific steps that should be taken:

1. If you are male or a non-menstruating female, take an oral mercury thermometer that has been shaken down below 95 degrees and placed at the bedside the previous evening. When you wake up, place the thermometer under your arm with the bulb in the armpit and no clothing between it and the armpit for 10 minutes. This reading taken in the armpit is somewhat lower and somewhat more accurate than by mouth. Repeat the test five days in a row. This is known as your Early AM Basal Temperature. Normal temperature ranges from 97.8 degrees to 98.2 degrees. If your temperature is low, your thyroid gland is probably underactive.

2. If you are a female who menstruates, do the above test on the second and third day of your period in the same manner.
3. If you have a very young child and are unable to take his/her armpit temperature, you can take the rectal temperature for two minutes. Normal would be 1 degree higher than the above—that is 98.8 degrees to 99.2 degrees.
4. Record your results below and bring this record to your physician.

RESULTS	TEMPERATURE
Date:_____	Day 1: _____
Date:_____	Day 2: _____
Date:_____	Day 3: _____
Date:_____	Day 4: _____
Date:_____	Day 5: _____

This temperature test is not part of what is considered the standard diagnosis of low thyroid. Nevertheless, if you consistently get a reading that is well below the normal range, the evidence is pointing to a sluggish metabolism. Consistently low temperatures, especially in someone who has some of the other symptoms and a family history of low thyroid, can be quite compelling evidence.

If your Barnes Basal Temperature Test reveals a consistently below-normal temperature, ask your physician for more than the usual thyroid panel of tests. Ask for the TSH (thyroid stimulating hormone) test, which is a more accurate index of thyroid functions. If your blood tests are normal, but you haven't been tested for thyroid antibodies, insist on this as a next step. So you have several potential steps.

But remember: the greatest test is how you feel.

TREATMENT OF HYPOTHYROIDISM

IF YOU HAVE SYMPTOMS OF HYPO-THYROIDISM, I recommend that you first take the "Liver Cleanse" that is described below. It is remarkable how much difference a clean liver makes in many, many people who suffer from low thyroid.

An excellent way to stimulate the liver to detoxify itself is with coffee enemas. We refer to this as a "Liver Cleanse." They are not for the function of cleansing the intestines. This enema is most often used in metabolic cancer therapy and is extremely valuable in many successful detoxification programs. Enema bags are available in any drugstore. One word of medical caution—enemas tend to delete the potassium level, therefore care must be taken for proper supplementation.

Coffee enemas alkalinize the first part of the intestines, enhance enzyme function, and stimulate the production and release of bile.

The coffee is absorbed through the colon wall and travels via the portal vein directly to the liver. When it stimulates the liver to produce bile, it can cause nausea. A little nausea is desirable, but if it is too great, reduce the amount of coffee used or use the enema on a full stomach. The coffee should be stronger than for drinking. Do not dilute the coffee.

The type of coffee to be used is ground (drip) coffee, not instant or decaffeinated. Mix 2 tablespoons of coffee to 1 quart of steam-distilled water. Use 2 cups at body temperature, twice daily. Take this enema preferably on your knees or lie down on your back, legs drawn close to abdomen, and breathe deeply while the enema is given slowly. Retain the fluid for 10 to 15 minutes.

To detoxify the liver in serious conditions, take two coffee enemas per day. Follow this routine for two weeks, then coffee enemas should be reduced to only one per week for one month.

Your body may have a buildup of toxins or poisons from time to time. Symptoms indicating toxicity are a decrease in appetite, headaches, increase in tiredness, and a general lack of well-being. When these occur, increase coffee enemas once again to one per day until symptoms subside or for a maximum of three to four days.

I also recommend a liver dysfunction diet, which is designed to bring healing to the liver. It must contain high-quality protein, such as white turkey meat, leg of lamb, wild game, white low-fat cheese, yogurt, cottage cheese, goat's milk, sprouted seeds and grains, raw nuts (especially almonds), and sesame butter or ground sesame seeds sprinkled over food, raw and steamed vegetables of all kinds.

Small, frequent meals are preferred rather than two or three large ones. Raw, fresh vegetables and fruits, free of artificial colors, preservatives, or chemicals of any kind are a must. Avoid all animal fats, canned and refined foods, synthetic vitamins, drugs, strong spices, sugar, coffee, black tea, and alcohol.

The best juices at this time are carrot/celery/parsley with one teaspoon of cream for every eight ounces of juice, red beet (excellent), cucumber, papaya, blue grapes, lemon, and green juice. The best herbs are dandelion, St. John's Wort, lobelia, parsley, horsetail, birch leaves, and sarsaparilla. The best herb teas are peppermint, spearmint, chamomile, thyme, milk thistle, and licorice.

If the symptoms continue, I recommend that you go to a doctor. Similar to the relationship of insulin and a diabetic, a small amount of thyroid hormone must be supplied from the outside to make up for the shortfall when a person's thyroid function is deficient and the gland is not responding adequately. For the majority of patients with hypothyroidism, taking some form of thyroid hormone replacement returns the thyroid blood tests to the normal range. While there are several synthetic thyroxines available, I strongly recommend Armour thyroid, which is a natural thyroid drug.

This process does not always work smoothly for every patient, and if you're one of them, it is very important to find a doctor or specialist who will listen and be sympathetic. Because most patients improve when sufficient thyroid hormone is provided, physicians often rely solely on test results to determine when a patient is on the appropriate dose. If you're still feeling the symptoms, talk with your doctor.

Thyroid Boosters
Iodine

A goiter may be caused by a lack of iodine, which causes the thyroid to swell. With today's emphasis on staying "off table salt," which contains added iodine, it's possible to push your iodine intake down too low. Taking kelp, a natural form of iodine, will stimulate the thyroid into producing more thyroid hormone.

Natural Glandular Support

Most nutrition stores carry what is called a natural thyroid glandular. Although they do not contain the thyroid hormone and are considered nutritional products, their use borders on the medicinal. They usually come in tablet form and consist of freeze-dried purified animal glands, with their associated hormones removed. For some people they apparently provide just enough support to the thyroid gland to stimulate adequate hormone production.

Essential Fatty Acids

Essential fatty acids (1,000 to 1,500 mg) are necessary for optimal hormone production.

It may be wise to avoid flaxseed oil due to high levels of cyanogenic glycosides. A better choice for the hypothyroid patient is cold water fish oils, which provide Omega 3 oils, and borage oil.

VITAMINS

A vitamin is a catalyst that enables other nutrients to work. Vitamin deficiencies can result in low thyroid. You must take a complete and high-quality multivitamin with minerals as a simple way of getting most of the nutrients your body requires. It is vital that you regularly take a balanced "stress" B-complex (50 to 100 mg/day) with meals, which improves cellular oxygenation and energy. Vitamin B12 in particular should be taken in lozenges several times a day.

Vitamin C (1,000 mg) is vital for the immune system and can facilitate the production of the thyroid hormone. Its antioxidant properties alone make it an excellent additive for thyroid sufferers. Vitamin E (400 IU/day) is another excellent antioxidant. A person with low thyroid cannot convert beta-carotene into Vitamin A, and when the body is low in Vitamin A (10,000 to 25,000 IU/day) it cannot produce the thyroid stimulating hormone (TSH). A deficiency in Vitamin A also reduces the ability of the thyroid to take up iodine. Fish liver oil is an excellent source to add Vitamin A to your daily intake.

MINERALS

Minerals, particularly selenium, copper, and zinc, are vital to healthy thyroid function. Minerals function, along with vitamins, as components of body enzymes. They are important to the production of hormones and enzymes and in the creation of antibodies. Selenium (200 mcg/day) is thought to support the vital conversion of T-4 (thyroxine) into T-3 (thyronine) and is also found in tuna, mushrooms, and wheat germ. Calcium (1,000 mg/day) suppresses a fat-storing parathyroid hormone—a hormone that's often poorly regulated in thyroid conditions—and has been shown in a Purdue University study to help weight loss when taken regularly. Make sure your mineral supplements are at the levels they need to be. Another way to boost your system is by adding some sea vegetables to your diet.

L-Tyrosine

This amino acid is the basis for the thyroid hormones thyroxin and triodothyronine. T-3 and T-4 are made of three or four atoms respectively of iodine attached to the tyrosine molecule. Tyrosine supplementation (500 mg), when health is good and iodide intake is adequate, may increase thyroid hormone levels.

Herbs

A liquid bladder wrack—an old herbal remedy—is very natural to the body and excellent for speeding up the metabolism with no harmful side effects. I have found it particularly effective for patients on a weight-loss program. A combination of herbs rich in minerals, such as horsetail, oatstraw, alfalfa, and gotu kola, will support thyroid function. Irish Moss, two or three times daily, is also good. While the most commonly used herbs do not comprehensively deal with low thyroid, they can be useful in easing many of the individual symptoms of low thyroid. Herbal energy boosters do not address the specific thyroid problem. And a few herbal stimulants, such as ma-huang, guarana, and excessive caffeine, cause stress to the thyroid and adrenals and should be avoided.

RECOMMENDED FOODS

"For people with an underactive thyroid, eating high-fiber foods or taking a fiber supplement can help their condition," says Mary Shomon, author of *The Thyroid Diet Guide*. Fiber picks up the slack for a sluggish metabolism, binding to food and moving it quickly through our system so we absorb fewer calories. One study showed that individuals absorbed 130 fewer calories on days when they increased their fiber intake from 18 grams to 36 grams. Shomon's Web site (www.thyroid-info.com) says that high-fiber favorites such as vegetables, berries, and popcorn are all part of her thyroid-boosting plan.

Tyrosine, a micronutrient found in certain types of protein, such as dairy products, partners with iodine to help the thyroid manufacture thyroid hormone. If you're avoiding dairy foods in favor of supplements, the only way to get enough tyrosine is to eat "a serving of beans or fish," says Jerry Hickey, R.Ph., of the

Society of Natural Pharmacy. When you get enough tyrosine and iodine, your metabolism operates at peak form.

I have dedicated an entire chapter in my book, *How to Feel Great All the Time,* to what I consider the best diet for your overall health, which is the Levitical Diet. You want to avoid as many refined and chemically tainted foods as possible—these disrupt vital organ functions, including the thyroid. I always recommend fresh, whole, organic foods whenever possible. Eat lots of egg yolks, parsley, apricots, dates, prunes, and fish. Dedicate yourself to a nutrient-rich diet that is low in fat, high in protein, low in sugar, and high in complex carbohydrates. Especially as regards the thyroid hormone, try to purchase meat from range-fed cattle and poultry raised on an organic diet. Avoid as much as possible the harmful hormone-blockers or hormone-mimics that confuse the body's immune system.

You must decrease the amount of fat in your diet, which is doable if you simply move to a healthy balanced diet of whole foods. I recommend that thyroid patients not skip breakfast, especially because the early morning is when certain hormones are at the high point in their daily cycle. Food intake becomes all that more important during this time. I also recommend that you begin your day with a meal that stimulates your metabolic activity— such as a high-protein smoothie and hot cereal with whole grain toast.

WHAT TO AVOID

It should go without saying that anyone with low thyroid needs to avoid whatever harms the body. In particular, tobacco, alcohol, sugar, and caffeine are at the top of the list. Nicotine impairs the conversion of T-3 to T-4. Avoid fried foods and fast foods, hydrogenated vegetable oils, and Aspartame (Equal/Nutrasweet).

There are a surprising number of foods, many of them otherwise very nutritious, that can adversely affect thyroid levels. Certain vegetables from the cabbage family cause a swelling of the thyroid gland (goitrogenic) and should be avoided—Brussel sprouts, broccoli, cabbage, cauliflower, mustard greens, horse-radish, radish, kohlrabi, white mustard, turnips, spinach, rutabaga, and kale. These have been shown to interfere with one's normal thyroid hormone production. Similarly, eating large quantities of almonds, walnuts, pine nuts, peanuts, sorghum, and millet can also stimulate the release of substances that may form goitrogens in the body. Peaches and pears should only be eaten in moderation.

TIME TO TRAIN

As your thyroid function improves, so will your energy levels. Now's the time to take advantage of that long-lost energy by exercising more, which will help your thyroid function even better and boost your energy even higher. Low thyroid results in the reduction of the release of serotonin—the feel-good hormone—which can contribute to depression and feelings of lethargy. Exercise helps push the levels of serotonin and improves your mood and energy, *besides* burning calories.

So are you ready to start? Go to Chapter Four, "Exercise and Water," in my book, *How to Feel Great All the Time,* and be prepared to turn the corner on how you feel and look.

FASTING

ALONG WITH THE "LIVER CLEANSE" THAT I've already described, fasting is a powerful tool that will help keep your thyroid gland functioning at peak performance. Fasting is a period of restricted food intake that detoxifies the body, giving the organs a rest and bringing natural healing by cleansing the body. But fasting is not only excellent for the body, it is also breath to the spirit as well. God says in Isaiah 58 that He has a chosen fast that is redemptive for every area of your life. Your spirit, mind, and body are included so that no disease will come upon you! Fasting facilitates this divine freedom. "Then your light will break forth like the dawn, and your healing will quickly appear." Your fast can be a time to be restored to a right relationship with Him! He will go before you as your righteousness, and His glory will be your guardian.

Fasting has been practiced for centuries among many societies, particularly for religious purposes. Among the Jews, the Day of Atonement was the most prominent occasion for a public fast (Leviticus 16:29-31; 23:27-36; Numbers 29:7). The Old Testament also refers to many special fasts, both public and individual (Judges 20:26; 1 Samuel 14:24; 31:13; 2 Samuel 1:12; 12:16-23; 1 Kings 21:27; 2 Chronicles 20:3). Jesus Christ was led by the Spirit to a forty day and night fast in the desert, which was followed by a time of intense temptation (Matthew 4:1-11). He gave His followers instructions for how He wanted them to fast (Matthew 6:16-18), and there is clear evidence of fasting in the early church (Acts 13:2-3; 14:23).

WHAT ARE THE BENEFITS?

I have seen in my fasting and Candida clinic that fasting is both a primary means of detoxifying the body, shedding unwanted pounds, and a wonderful aid to spiritual renewal. While our emphasis for purposes of feeling great focuses on the cleansing of the body and weight loss, keep in mind that the health of your spiritual life is intrinsic to your overall health. There is no substitute for experiencing on a daily basis the fullness of joy from being in a right relationship with God.

Fasting has been proven to be the most effective means of getting the body into a natural healing process. It is also an instrument to literally reset the body's odometer and help reverse the aging process. Disease and aging begin when the normal process of cell regeneration and rebuilding slows down. This slowdown is caused by the accumulation of waste products in the tissues, which interferes with the nourishment and oxygenation of cells. This may happen at any age, and when it occurs, the cells' resistance to disease diminishes and various ills start to appear. Given the fact that at any given moment one-fourth of all our cells are dead and in replacement, it is of vital importance that the dying cells are decomposed and eliminated from the system as efficiently as possible. Quick and effective elimination of dead cells stimulates the building and growth of new cells.

Hippocrates (c. 460-377 B.C.), the Greek physician often called "the father of medicine," spoke of this well over two thousand years ago. He said, "Food should be our medicine, and medicine should be our food, but to eat when you are sick is to feed your illness." Such ancient advice contains true wisdom. When you stop eating, your organs rest, and all the energy in your body is directed to healing.

By ridding the body of toxicity, you will find yourself more alert and energetic, requiring less sleep, and you will experience a keener sense of awareness to those around you as well as to your own spirit and the Holy Spirit. In simple words, you will find yourself being led by your spirit and not by your appetite.

In Germany, Dr. Otto Buchinger Jr., who is an authority on fasting, has supervised over 90,000 successful fasting and detox programs and has used these methods to treat virtually every disease—rheumatic conditions, digestive disorders, skin conditions, cardiovascular disorders, and more. Diminished hormone levels can be restored simply by cleansing the body.

We now know that by fasting only three days a month, you can increase your life span by five to seven years. An interesting study was conducted in Europe with centenarians (those living to be over one hundred years of age). The study showed that there was only one common link among this age group—they all ate less than the average person, and they fasted often! Cornell University studies have shown that by keeping animals from overeating and implementing systematic fasting, their lives can be increased up to 50 percent.

HOW FASTING WORKS

Fasting means to not eat, but it doesn't mean you should restrict yourself to water only. In fact, juice fasting has proven to be the most effective way to restore your health back to the way God intended.

During a prolonged fast (after the first three days), your body will live on its own substance. When it is deprived of needed nutrition, particularly of proteins and fats, it will burn and digest its own tissues by the process of autolysis, or self-digestion. But your body will not do this indiscriminately! Through the divine wisdom of our Great Creator, your body will first decompose and burn those cells and tissues that are diseased, damaged, aged, or dead. In the fasting process, your body feeds itself on the most impure and inferior materials, such as dead cells and morbid accumulations—tumors, abscesses, fat deposits, etc. Dr. Buchinger says, "Fasting is a refuse disposal, a burning of rubbish." The essential body tissues and vital organs, the glands, the nervous system, and the brain are not damaged or digested in a fast.

In general, three- to ten-day fasts are recommended for health and longevity. The body needs three to five days of fasting to actually begin the autolysis process whereby the body attacks inferior matter in the body and begins the healing process. A five-day fast essentially clears debris before disease gets started. A ten-day fast works to attack disease that has already begun and often eliminates problems from the body before the symptoms arise. During the fast, the function of the eliminative organs—liver, kidneys, lungs, and the skin—is greatly increased, and accumulated toxins and waste are quickly expelled. During the fast, toxins in the urine can be ten times higher than normal.

HOW TO FAST

If you have never fasted before, it is best to start with several one-day fasts before moving on to a three-day fast. Do these once a week until you feel comfortable moving on.

Then have a three-day fast once a month. As a preparation for it, reduce the amount of food and eat only whole raw organic foods two to three days before you begin your fast. I recommend beginning the fast on a Friday evening and extending it through Monday evening. Most people are at home on weekends and can easily do their juicing and cleansing with few interruptions. For many people the second day feels the worst, so it's best to have that on a day of rest. Think of it as a time to give your body a rest, to let it retune itself, and to aid in its healing process.

Start each day of your fast with room temperature steam-distilled water. Every day you should be drinking half of your body weight in ounces of water. For example, if you weigh 150 pounds, drink 75 ounces of water each day. Health science consensus currently believes that steam-distilled water is the best for fasting as well as daily use. Steam-distilled water is the only water that actually goes in and pulls out toxins from the organs. It literally pulls out the mire that gets caught in the follicles of the colon and breeds disease. You will also find that steam-distilled water helps curb your appetite, unlike drinks or juice that causes your body to want more.

The best juices are the ones you juice yourself. Fresh organic veggies are in supply at your local health food store as well as grocery stores. Stock up on the freshest you can find. During a fast, my favorite juice is a carrot, beet, and ginger combination. Feel free to use a variety of veggies and fruits. Fresh lemon, cabbage, beet, carrot, grape (including the seeds), apple (skin and seeds), green combos made from leafy greens such as spinach, kale, turnips, etc.—these are all excellent detoxifiers.

Raw cabbage juice is known to aid in the recovery from ulcers, cancer, and all colon problems. However, it must be fresh, not stored. Cabbage loses its Vitamin U content after sitting for only a short time.

Another excellent juice blend is three carrots, two stalks of celery, one turnip, two beets, a half head of cabbage, a quarter bunch of parsley, and a clove of garlic. This could be one of the best juices on our planet for the restoration of the body from many ailments.

Another favorite juice preparation is Stanley Borroughs's "Master Cleanser." In a gallon of steam-distilled water, mix the juice of five fresh lemons and a half cup of grade B maple syrup. Add one or more tablespoons of hot cayenne pepper (at least 90,000 heat units) to your taste tolerance. This is especially good for alkalinizing the body and raising body temperature to help resolve infection and flu-type illnesses.

Pure vegetable broths with no seasonings added are also good. To prepare these, gently boil vegetables, including lots of onions and garlic, for 30 minutes. Do not eat the stew, but strain the broth and drink the juice two or three times a day.

The juices, broths, and water will keep you adequately full as well as provide you with more nutrients than most people normally get from their diets. If you must eat something, have a slice of watermelon. Organic grapes with seeds are also good, especially Concord grapes, which have a powerful antioxidant effect. Alternatively, fresh applesauce made with the skins on and the seeds intact, processed in a blender or food processor, is satisfying and won't significantly disrupt your fast.

A great way to top off your day, whether fasting or not, is to have a half cup of oat bran with a non-dairy milk (soy, almond, or rice). This helps to cleanse the colon by adding fiber and has been shown to cut the risk of cancer by 30 percent! I have found that eating oat bran before going to bed suits my body well and seems to aid in a peaceful night's rest.

Green drinks can also be an added bonus to any fast. We have created one called Creation's Bounty, which is a whole raw organic food with all the nutrients your body needs. There may also be other green drinks to choose from at your local health food store.

Daily Suggested Protocol for Your Fast

- Start with 4-8 ounces of Clustered Water™. This will help to clean the lymphatic system.
- Fifteen minutes later take 1-2 ounces of Body Oxygen™.
- Thirty to forty minutes later have a green drink.
- Prepare your favorite fresh juice combination, which you can alternate with

Stanley Burroughs's lemonade drink. If you don't have a juicer, use the best organic juice from your grocery store.

- Prepare fresh vegetables broth to sip in between juices and/or green smoothies.
- Remember to drink as much steam-distilled water as possible.
- A good liquid mineral supplement will aid in rapid healing.
- If you must eat, remember—grapes, watermelon, or fresh applesauce.
- Rest whenever you feel weak during a fast. Deep-breathing exercises and frequent showers are helpful.

FASTING DON'TS

- Don't fast on water alone!
- Don't chew gum or mints. This starts the digestive juices flowing and is harmful to the system. When your stomach releases hydrochloric acid in the gut, but nothing ever gets down there, is it a surprise that you have a stomachache?
- Don't drink orange or tomato juice on a fast. They are too acidic.

■ Don't ever eat junk foods, especially before the fast. The last food you eat will be the next food you crave. If you eat junk food, you'll want more of it. If you eat veggies, you'll want something healthy. Our bodies are designed by God to want healthy food, but when we eat the wrong things, we deaden our senses to what is good. Did you ever notice when you eat a fast-food burger you feel full for about 30 minutes, and then suddenly you're hungry again! This is because your body is so desperate for nutrition it is still trying to get you to eat something it can actually benefit from instead of dead, unbeneficial calories?

WHILE YOU FAST

When going on a juice fast of three days or longer, some experts advise taking an herbal laxative on the first day of the fast and every two or three days during a longer fast. I prefer and personally recommend enemas during a fast as an absolute must. Enemas assist the body in its detoxifying effort by cleansing out all the toxic waste from the alimentary canal.

A healthy, normal adult is carrying around 7-14 pounds of waste (that's the weight of a newborn baby!). Think of what an immune-compromised or overweight person may have stored up. People continually ask me why they are still having large bowel movements after several days of not eating. The answer is simple—most people have years of backup to clean out.

Enemas should be taken at least once, preferably twice, a day during your fast—one after rising in the morning and the other before going to bed. One pint to one quart of lukewarm distilled water is sufficient. One word of medical caution—enemas tend to delete the potassium level, therefore care must be taken for proper supplementation.

Although naturopaths have used both enemas and colonic irrigation for many years in their detoxification methods, its use is not without controversy. Fiber supplements are now available that can be taken by mouth and achieve similar purposes.

MAINTENANCE AFTER A FAST

Fasting brings the body back to doing what it is designed to do, which is for you to accomplish the will of God without the hindrances of fatigue, obesity, and illness. Most people, following initial withdrawal from chemical dependencies (including caffeine and sugar), dramatically see and feel a difference in their health status by day three of a good fast. People commonly feel lighter and more energized and notice improvements in complexion and eye color. These changes indicate you are on your way back to optimal health.

Always break the fast gently. Whole raw organic foods may be used. Nothing heavy or chemical laden should be eaten, such as processed foods. For powerful aid in rebuilding the immune system before and after the fast, drink Pau d'arco and Echinacea tea mixed with one-third unsweetened cranberry juice four times a day.

Lightly steamed vegetables in their broth with whole grain brown rice can be added slowly and used as part of a maintenance diet.

DEALING WITH THE HEALING CRISIS

When you alter your diet, especially during a fast, changes occur that are often misunderstood. Far too often I have seen individuals who were properly detoxing, cleansing, and healing quit just before the finish line. This is simply due to misunderstanding the way the body was designed by God to heal itself. The following will hopefully give you clarity as to what to expect when you are in the eliminative process that brings healing. Remember, the Word says, "At the proper time we will reap a harvest if we do not give up" (Galatians 6:9).

Dr. Bernard Jensen has defined a healing crisis as "an acute reaction resulting from the ascendance of the natural healing forces over disease conditions. Its tendency is toward recovery, and it is, therefore, in conformity with the natural reconstruction principle put innately in us by God." It is the direct result of an industrious effort of every organ in the body to eliminate waste products and set the stage for regeneration. Through this constructive process toward health, old tissues are replaced with new.

In a healing crisis there is usually a fever, which shows that the body is fighting to burn out residues of old viruses, bacteria, and disease in general. Symptoms of the healing crisis may at first be identical to the disease it is meant to heal. But the real distinction is elimination. Elimination is usually significantly increased, due to the fact that all the eliminative organs are doing their part to rid the body of harmful toxins and buildup. This is just the opposite in a diseased state, when the body is usually either constipated or very irregular, leaving the body in an unsatisfactory condition and compounding the trouble. When elimination occurs, you know that the body is in a purifying and cleansing process.

In time the new tissue becomes strong enough to take its place in the various activities of the body. The old tissue is expelled through various means—phlegm, mucous, sweat, bowels, etc. As the process of building up new cellular structure has been accomplished, the real healing is taking place.

According to Dr. Jensen, there are three stages to the healing crisis:

■ Eliminative—the body ridding itself of debris.

■ Transitional—new tissue is maturing.

■ Building—the body is then going into homeostasis, a state of health, the way God intended us to live.

A healing crisis usually lasts about three days. During that time, various aches, pains, and symptoms of ailments from long ago seem to rear their ugly head. Some people only experience a slight headache, while others may feel as if they are on their last leg. All of this is dependent upon the degree of cleansing the body needs to accomplish. If the crisis is bearable, work through it, as the rewards are well worth it. If it is unbearable, back off slightly, then try again later. The body will order each step of the crisis from the inside out and from the head down, which is why it usually starts with a headache.

Please keep in mind that the majority of physical problems the average American is facing is brought on by a poor diet, lack of exercise, and a fast-pace stressful lifestyle. Fasting and detoxing assist in ridding the body of the lifestyle buildups that eventually develop into chronic diseases. One healing crisis may not be enough for complete restoration. You may require a number of cycles of healing crises. Think of it as peeling the layers off an onion.

Keep in mind that the crisis is necessary in order for true healing to take place. You must get rid of the old to bring in the new. Just think of the whole body getting into action to correct ailing organs, joints, and various conditions in the body. True healing can never occur without a real cleansing of the eliminative organs.

After the healing crisis has occurred, strength, energy, and health begin to build. After a cleanse, a healthy diet, proper amounts of oxygen, good water and lots of it, along with a moderate exercise program, you will be giving your body what it needs to stay on track.

As always, you may want to consult your physician regarding any concerns you have about symptoms during what you perceive to be a healing crisis. It is easy to mistake serious medical symptoms for minor symptoms. And always check with your physician before beginning any new cleansing or exercise program.

VALERIE SAXION'S
SILVER CREEK LABS

THROUGHOUT THIS BOOKLET, I HAVE NOTED FOUR PRODUCTS that will aid you in your detoxification efforts as well as pro- mote a healthy body. To order these products or to contact Silver Creek Laboratories for a complete catalog and order form of other nutritional supplements and health products, call (817) 236-8557, toll free at (800) 493- 1146, fax (817) 236-5411, or write us at:

9555 Harmon Road
Fort Worth, TX 76177.

Body Oxygen. A pleasant-tasting nutritional supplement that is meticulously manufac- tured with cold pressed aloe vera. The aloe is used as a stabilized carrier for numerous nutri- tional constituents, including magnesium per- oxide and pure anaerocidal oxygen, haw- thorne berry, ginkgo biloba, ginseng, and St. John's Wort. It helps naturally fight infections, inflammation, and degeneration by taking oxygen in at the cellular level. It also commonly helps in colon cleansing, regular elimination, and provides a feeling of increased energy and mental alertness.

Candida Cleanse. A decade in coming, this is the most powerful natural agent I know of in the fight against *Candida*. It is specifically formulated for TOTAL *Candida* cleansing. A two-part system is also available to rid the body of *Candida* and parasites called *ParaCease*.

Dr. Lorenzen's Clustered Water is probably the greatest breakthrough in health science product development in this century. Clustered Water, produced at home using one ounce of solution to one gallon of steam-distilled water, replenishes the most vital support for all cellular DNA and the 4,000 plus enzymes that are involved in every metabolic process in your body. This amazing product increases nutrient absorption by up to 600 percent, which means your vitamins and organic foods will deliver far more vital nutrients to your body. It replicates the powerful healing waters of the earth! Excellent for cleaning out lymphatic fluids! It comes in a C-400 formula for those who are generally healthy and detoxed, and a SBX formula for the immune-compromised.

Creation's Bounty. Simply the best, pleasant-tasting, green, whole, raw, organic food supplement available—a blend of whole, raw, organic herbs and grains, principally amaranth, brown rice, spirulina, and flaxseed. This combination of live foods with live enzymes assists your body in the digestion of foods void of enzymes. You will gain vital nutrients, protein, carbohydrates, and good fats to nourish your body and brain, resulting in extra energy and an immunity boost as well. It is a whole food, setting it apart from other green foods on the market.

Unleash Your Greatness

AT BRONZE BOW PUBLISHING WE ARE COMMITTED

to helping you achieve your ultimate potential

in functional athletic strength, fitness, natural

muscular development, and all-around superb

health and youthfulness.

Our books, videos, newsletters, Web sites, and training seminars will bring you the very latest in scientifically validated information that has been carefully extracted and compiled from leading scientific, medical, health, nutritional, and fitness journals worldwide.

Our goal is to empower you! To arm you with the best possible knowledge in all facets of strength and personal development so that you can make the right choices that are appropriate for *you*.

Now, as always, **the difference between greatness and mediocrity** begins with a choice. It is said that knowledge is power. But that statement is a half truth. Knowledge is power only when it has been tested, proven, and applied to your life. At that point knowledge becomes wisdom, and in wisdom there truly is *power*. The power to help you choose wisely.

So join us as we bring you the finest in health-building information and natural strength-training strategies to help you reach your ultimate potential.

FOR INFORMATION ON ALL OUR EXCITING NEW SPORTS AND FITNESS PRODUCTS, CONTACT:

BRONZE BOW PUBLISHING
2600 East 26th Street
Minneapolis, MN 55406

WEB SITES
www.bronzebowpublishing.com
www.masterlevelfitness.com

612.724.8200   Toll Free **866.724.8200**   FAX **612.724.8995**